NOTE TO PARENTS

Apologetics Press is a non-profit organization dedicated to the defense of New Testament Christianity. For over 35 years, we have provided faith-building materials for adults. We also have produced numerous materials for young people of all ages.

The Apologetics Press Early Reader Series is a set of books aimed at children in kindergarten through second grade. Depending on the age of your children, this series is flexible enough to allow parents to read to their children, read along with their children, or listen while their children read aloud to them.

The books in this series are filled with beautiful, full-color pictures and wonderful information about God, His creation, and His Word. These books are written on a level that early readers will enjoy, while drawing them closer to their Creator.

We hope you enjoy using the Apologetics Press Early Reader Series to encourage your children to read, while at the same time helping them learn about God and His creation.

See also our Learn to Read Series
for 3-6 year olds and our Advanced
Reader Series for 2nd-3rd graders.
www.ApologeticsPress.org
(800) 234-8558

God Made You

by Kyle Butt

Copyright © 2012
(reprint 2016)
Apologetics Press

ISBN-13: 978-1-60063-054-5

Library of Congress: 2012940636

Printed in China

God Made You

by Kyle Butt

God made you. You did not evolve over millions of years.

You are not an accident.

God gave you many wonderful parts.

One of those parts is your brain.

God designed your brain to work
like a very fast computer.
It can store lots of information.

It controls your lungs, heart, and other organs.

You don't even have to think about making your heart beat. Your brain does that for you.

God also made your eyes. They are amazing as well.

Your eyes are like cameras
that take pictures of things
around you.

They send these pictures
to your brain.
Your brain then lets you
know what you are seeing.

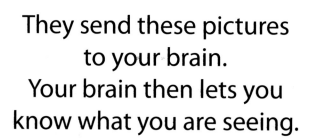

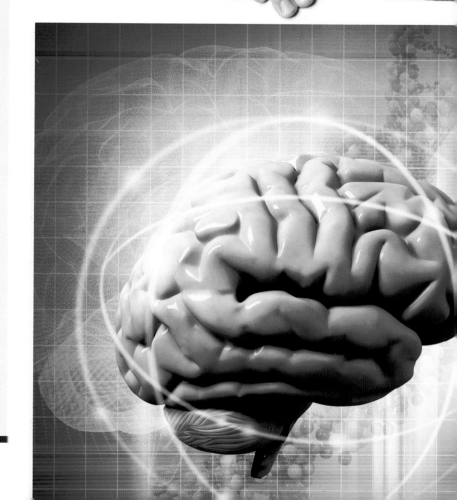

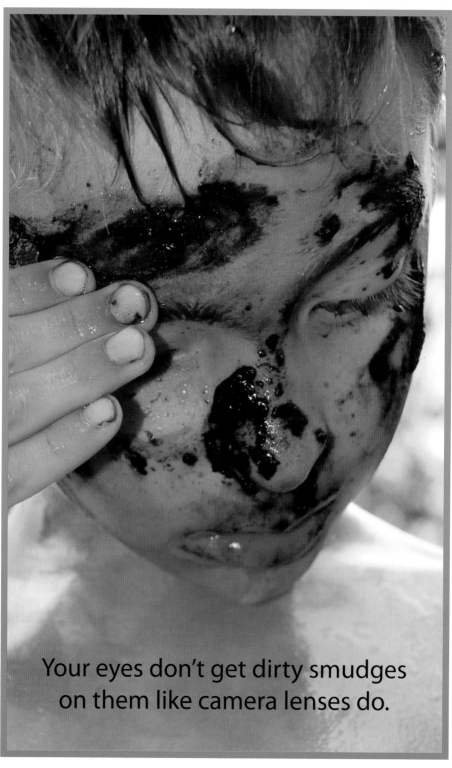

Your eyes don't get dirty smudges on them like camera lenses do.

Your eyelids wash them when you blink.

If you look in the mirror, what else do you see?
For one thing, you see your ears.

God designed your ears to hear. Your ears have a special piece of skin inside them called an eardrum.

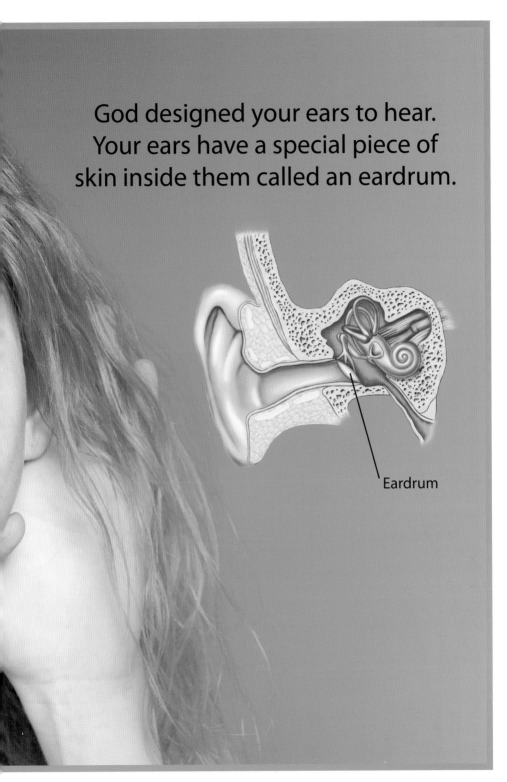

Eardrum

Your eardrums pick
up vibrations.
These vibrations are
turned into sounds.

You also have a wonderful
tongue. Your tongue helps
you taste food.
It helps you talk and swallow.

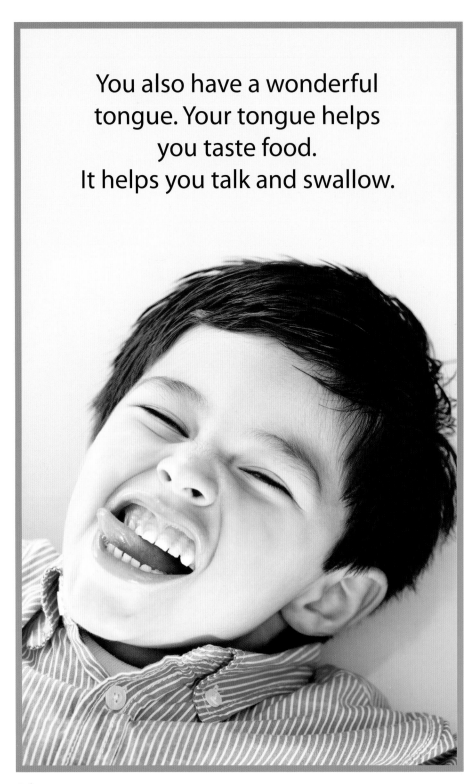

What is just above your mouth?

That's right, your nose.
Your nose helps you smell when
something is rotten or tasty.

Your skin is also a wonderful and important part of your body.

goosebumps

It protects your body from
harmful germs.

Your skin also has nerves in it.
Nerves help you feel sensations like
hot, cold, wet, and dry.

Only God could design your amazing body. Be sure to thank Him for it.